BLAZERS

Wild Outdoors

Camping

by Cindy Jenson-Elliott

Reading Consultant: Barbara J. Fox
Reading Specialist
North Carolina State University

Content Consultant: Karen Snodgrass
National Youth Director
Family Campers and RVers

CAPSTONE PRESS
a capstone imprint

Blazers is published by Capstone Press,
151 Good Counsel Drive, P.O. Box 669, Mankato, Minnesota 56002.
www.capstonepub.com

Books published by Capstone Press are manufactured with paper
containing at least 10 percent post-consumer waste.

Library of Congress Cataloging-in-Publication Data
Jenson-Elliott, Cindy L.
  Camping / by Cindy Jenson-Elliott.
    p. cm. — (Blazers. Wild outdoors)
  Summary: "Describes the equipment, skills, and knowledge needed for camping"—Provided by
publisher.
  Includes bibliographical references and index.
  ISBN 978-1-4296-4812-7 (library binding)
  1. Camping—Juvenile literature. I. Title.
  GV191.7.J46 2012
  796.54—dc22   2011003778

Editorial Credits
Angie Kaelberer, editor; Gene Bentdahl, designer; Sarah Schuette,
     photo stylist; Marcy Morin, scheduler; Eric Manske, production specialist

Photo Credits
Capstone Studio: Karon Dubke, 14–15; Corbis: Ariel Skelley, 22–23; Dreamstime: Sergey
Zavalnyuk, 11 (top); iStockphoto: Danny Warren, cover, Isaac Koval, 26–27, Robert Churchill,
12 (front), 28–29, stockstudioX, 18–19, Vladimir Piskunov, 20–21; Shutterstock: Blend
Images, 18 (front), Bruce MacQueen, 4–5, Elena Elisseeva, 26 (front), IDAL, 21 (front), Linda
Armstrong, 17 (top), Maksym Gorpenyuk, 12–13, Mirek Srb, 6–7, Morgan Lane Photography,
10–11, oliveromg, 8–9, Robert Zywucki, 24, Rufous, 16–17

Artistic Effects
Capstone Studio: Karon Dubke (woods); Shutterstock: rvika (wood), rvrspb (fence),
VikaSuh (sign)

Printed in the United States of America in Stevens Point, Wisconsin.
032011   006111WZF11

Table of Contents

Chapter 1

Into the Wild

The morning is quiet. You sit by a campfire warming your hands on a cup of cocoa. Suddenly, you hear a stick snap. Two deer step into your campsite.

Wild Fact:

Early morning is a good time to see wildlife. Many animals look for food at that time of day.

Wild Fact:

Don't get too close to animals or try to feed them. They may attack if they feel threatened.

You and the deer stand still, eyes on each other. Then the deer turn and leap away. Being so close to nature is exciting! You never know what you will see when you camp.

Chapter 2

Pack Up!

People camp in **wilderness** areas or campgrounds. They bring everything they need with them. Most campers bring a tent, sleeping bags, food, and cooking equipment.

wilderness—a wild place in nature without many people

Campers sleep in tents made of strong, lightweight nylon. In wet weather, a **fly** on top of the tent keeps out rain. Sleeping bags keep campers warm inside the tent.

fly—waterproof tent cover

fly

For comfort, a tent should hold
the number of campers, plus one.

Many campers say food tastes best outdoors. They cook meals over camp stoves or fires. They roast marshmallows and hot dogs on sticks.

Wild Fact:

Campfires are not allowed everywhere. Campers should check campground rules.

tent

warm clothing

gloves

sun hat

sunglasses

water bottle

insect repellent

first-aid kit

First Aid Kit

sleeping bag

sleeping pad

water tablets

soap

OFF!

skillet

stove and fuel

whistle

pocket knife

waterproof matches

14

Camping Equipment

backpack

food

camera

large garbage bags

lantern

cooler and ice

sunscreen

maps

compass

flashlight

Chapter 3

Skills and Techniques

A campsite should have a flat space for a tent and room for a campfire. Some campgrounds have bathrooms and running water. Others are **primitive**.

primitive—describes campgrounds with no bathrooms or running water

restroom

Wild Fact:

Some campgrounds charge fees to stay there. Others are free.

Campers bring their own water to primitive campsites. They also boil, filter, or **treat** water from natural sources. Untreated stream and lake water may contain germs that make people sick.

boiling water

treat—to kill germs by adding chemicals

water filter

Campfires make camping a cozy experience. At night, campers often sit around a fire to stay warm, talk, and sing. Campers build fires by piling **tinder**, sticks, and logs in loose layers.

tinder—small pieces of wood that catch fire easily

Chapter 4
Safety

Safe campers build fires away from trees, bushes, or tents. They always stay near their fires. Unattended campfires can start forest fires.

Wild Fact:

Make sure a fire is out at bedtime by pouring water on it.

Wild Fact:

Food and garbage attract animals. Store these items in a locked car or a bear box.

Campers respect nature. They haul out trash. They camp at least 100 feet (30 meters) from water sources. This distance keeps garbage and waste from **polluting** the water.

pollute—to make something dirty with waste or germs
bear box—a bear-resistant storage locker for food

Hiking in the woods is a fun part of camping. Safe campers avoid **poisonous** plants. Touching poison ivy and poison oak can cause a painful rash.

poison ivy

poisonous—able to cause harm

Chapter 5

Camping Out!

Away from city lights, campers enjoy the beauty of nature. Pack up your tent, and let's go camping!

Glossary

bear box (BAIR BOKS)—a bear-resistant storage locker for food

fly (FLYE)—a waterproof tent cover

poisonous (POI-zuhn-uhss)—able to kill or harm if swallowed, inhaled, or touched

pollute (puh-LOOT)—to make something dirty with waste or germs

primitive (PRIM-uh-tiv)—describes a campground with no bathrooms or running water

tinder (TIN-duhr)—small pieces of wood that catch fire easily

treat (TREET)—to kill germs by adding chemicals

wilderness (WIL-dur-niss)—a wild area where few or no people live

Read More

Champion, Neil. *Camping and Hiking.* Get Outdoors. New York: PowerKids Press, 2011.

Keller, Kristin Thoennes. *Camping.* The Great Outdoors. Mankato, Minn.: Capstone Press, 2008.

Studelska, Jana Voelke. *Camping for Fun.* For Fun. Mankato, Minn.: Capstone Press, 2008.

Internet Sites

FactHound offers a safe, fun way to find Internet sites related to this book. All of the sites on FactHound have been researched by our staff.

Here's all you do:

Visit *www.facthound.com*

Type in this code: 9781429648127

Index